I0080485

Tweets from a Wounded Nightingale

ALY SEBASTIAN

Tweets from a Wounded Nightingale

Copyright © 2015 Aly Sebastian

All rights reserved.

ISBN:069269434X
ISBN-13: 978-0692694343

FOR BRYNJOLF

"Our trinity serves the Lady Nocturnal, the Empress of Murk and the Daughter of Twilight. We believe her to be our patron, if not the patron of all thieves worldwide. We serve her without prayer, without charity and without celebration."
–Gallus Desidenius

Tweets from a Wounded Nightingale

Tweets from a Wounded Nightingale

Tweets from a Wounded Nightingale

ACKNOWLEDGMENTS

Thanks to Chanda Tan, Jay Sebastian, Sven Jorgenson,
Althea Terenzi, Tanya Valverde, Valerie Terenzi, Vanessa
Lyons, MaryJane Terenzi, Persephone, Karick, and Rowan.

In Memory of Harry Terenzi

Thanks to my online community. All the prompsters.
@MadQueenStorm @Madverse, @AshBahget @ashverse,
@CamWylde @wyldeverse, @fieryverse, @writtenriver,
@fridayphrases, @Pat_Sherard, @poetme13,
@chipmunkofpower, @clintingtons, @andynamp,
@awaitingfrost, @Lostsub50T, @BklynMercardo,
@thepunkdroet, @JDEstradawriter, @BettyElyazidi,
@rfolkard1, @kaygardnersdp, @bailseyface,
@a_hero_unlikely,@JaeDanzig, @OdinsKnot,
@EvilInnocentEye, @GeneVatow, @wordrefiner,
@Simpsondm7071, @AuthorTrandahl,
@Banquozghost, @RavensVeil, @scandy1029,
@PowerOfMyWords, @RichardLabbett,
@do_the_posture, @writingreader, @Morgaine620,
@bevandeviere, @wyattmcintire, @spartagus,
@_Sense_Wrds and all the others out there who have been
supportive and inspiring.

Tweets from a Wounded Nightingale

#AdviceFromaCrow

I

Sit on my shoulder

Grandmother Crow

There is so much

I wish to know

Will he be coming?

What is his name?

Will there be sunshine?

Will there be pain?

Tell me please

Wise old crone

Will I still love him

After he's gone?

II

Dear child of nature

Please listen and hear

There's much more to the future

B'sides those who are dear

Storms will brew

And winds will blow

Listen close to the love

Beneath blankets of snow

Hear the lessons

That come with the pain

There is no love

Without any rain

#LoveLetter

I wrote you a love letter

Inscribed it upon my skin

With blue ink and promises

Bonestain ennui seeping in

A tattoo you didn't care for

@ The Black Market

Like a whore

Masked as a lady

Shady back alley

Snakeoil dealings

Hope is gold

Sold my soul

Disabused notions

Useless potions

I never could fly

#IllusoryFreedom

Her soul was free to soar

But her heart was still chained

Remaining with long ago love

Forever cleaved in twain

#MytRustyBlade

Sword on my back

Trudging through snow

Alert for attack

Onward I go

Moon's unlawful light

Makes a last stand

Burden of Night

Blood on my hands

#ExistentialCrisis

Welcome! Do come in! Please join me for tea.

Perhaps share an existential crisis or three.

I'll be the hatter and you'll be the queen.

You can use flattery and I'll be terribly obscene.

We'll conversate on philosophy and have a debate

And hash out conundrums over crumpets and cakes.

We can expound and ponder the meaning of time.

And judge the merit of a poem's last line.

Sum up the universe in the last of the dregs.

And leave feeling stranger for having had met.

@ Dusk

Well hello my dear host

Let me just slip of this old thing

And into something a little more obscene

Less, confining, restraining, or binding

I emerge from the pages of my story

Into your head

Like slipping into the bed of a stranger

For one night of love

Dawn cracks your skull wide

Nothing inside

But you can't get rid of me

Still haunted by my ghost

#SuckYouBus

She comes on night's breath

To torture and tease

With nightsweat promises

Of deathsweet release

Mercurial lover

A sigh in his ear

She brings him to madness

To then disappear

#Monday

I skim the surface and hope that's enough.

Maybe I'd drown if I was allowed

In the deep end anyway.

Ashes & Dust

When I pass give my ashes unto the West Wind's
prodigious care

As you stand upon the four-corner crossroads wailing your farewell

Let me live on as the dust of aged books carried by whimsicality of air

To settle like inspiration in the nooks and pages where future writers dwell.

The Gift

When the voices tell you to stop writing
When the words are no longer delighting
When the agony becomes too much to bare
Know the gift of story is always there
When the rejections come in droves
When the plotlines have come unwove
When the characters hate you so
Know the gift of story will never go
When the time is scarce and the day Is long
When the grammar is off and the spelling wrong
When the twists and turns make you ill
Know the gift of story is there still
When the paper burns and the ink runs dry
When your lights go out and your laptop dies
When the universe hands you down a block
Know the gift of story cannot be stopped
So write on friends
There are stories to tell

You are born with a gift
Use that gift well

#BringerofAsh

On Black Mountain
Swords will clash
Armies lost
All hope dashed
With iron fist
Enemies smashed
Kneel down before
The Bringer of Ash

#LoveBites

Hypnotic stare
Night begins
Selfish impetus
Invited in
Passion intense
Cardinal sin
Love bites
Pulsing skin
Soft surrender
Evil wins

#Trolls

They scroll

Roll their eyes

No disguising

Their disdain

Inflicting pain

Impotent reign

Self-importance

Creating tension

For attention

#JaneAustin

I want to be Jane Austin

And throw away my sensibility

For any gentleman who comes to call

To fall in love with the nobility

And have my heart broken

By the inequity of it all

To put curious pen to parchment

Capture the fickleness of those who fall

I want to be Jane Austin

The girl who had the gall

#Numb

He was called a blasphemer

A disbeliever

If he couldn't touch

It wasn't real

So much love

He refused to feel

#Steam

Lost my train of thought

Tied to the tracks on your arm

A steampunk junkyard

#AmQuerying

Another rejection

Agents of dejection

Sorry

Wrong direction

Correction of hope

No affection

It's not a reflection

Dope book though

Keep querying

#CafeMochaWakefulness

Chocolate roses

Melting in my fingers

Coffee colored dream

Decadence lingers

A warm kiss of morning

Nudging me awake

#Chambord

"Chambord with this charade!"

Leaning heavy on the balustrade

Takes a glass from a passing maid

Slurring, "This is funny lemonade."

#Humans

If you see a drowning person,

Pull them from the pool.

One simple twist of fate,

And you could be that poor fool.

#ATisket

Leave a chocolate

Put in in a yellow basket

A little piece of hope

For the morning

Fertile imagination

Fed with sweets

A treat for the soul

#DoomSayer

Dark armies amass against the wall
Unebbing flow the tides of gloom
Betrayer of every king & thrall
Unprepared to meet their doom

#Tears

A pond fills with tears of regret
Goldfish swimming pirouettes
Frogprinces on lilypad ships of sunset
But alas she ever lacks a net

#prophecy

Her prophecies waxed poetic
Adorning frenetic horrors
Hearts sewn shut with threads of fate
Lacy destiny written in blood
Too late

#friends

Friends are like good coffee
The finest boldest roast
Fueling my energy & focus
I raise a mug to them in toast

#spiralingout

Mascara stained pillow
Weeping willow
Out on a limb
Haunted by him
Spirits swirling
Stomach sour
Drain tornado
Mourning shower

#April

Snowclad crocus
His focus
Spring feverdream
Twisting tendrils
Rising smoke
Sinking mire
Desirous flesh

Dewy brows
Earth aroused

#Easter

A path of eggshells in her wake
Eostre walks the fertile earth
Reminding us how easily we all break
From the outset of our birth

#science

Molecules of pain
In rain
Rivers rising over banks
To thank
Life's stormy pewter skies
Their cries
Quenching arid crops
teardrops

#spring

As above so below
Stormy skies
Full rainbow

Heavens fury
Melting snow
Reluctant hearts
Flowers grow
Dormant seeds
Love has sewn

#PennyforYourThoughts

Had a holy pocket
Fear fell out tumbling
Across the floor
Like loose change
How strange to see
Old currency unstored
Worthless

#MondayMusic

Flatblack circle
Spinning me rightround
Song of my youth
How my angst was drowned
Through the tip of a needle
Tattooing of sound

#FountainPens

The inktree slow drips
Black ruined portrait
Bleeding Belladonna lips
Dreaming love's hate
Poison petticoated hips
Darkly daybreak

#YarnBalls

Go ahead
Pull the thread
Unraveling my heart
Naked truth
Traveling a labyrinth
Of my soul
My goal
The smile
Of my inner child

#AmWriting

Words we write
Righting the past
Mystic incantation

True iconoclast
Blurring lines
Inked everlast
Love is reborn
In moments passed

#AllThatGlitters

Gilty pleasures
Moments treasured
Bold brush of fingertips
Midas touch of lips
Too precious to hold
Turning this moment to gold

@TheFullMoon

La triste lune
A wolf who lost his mate
Her countenance in the moon
Howling at the fates
She was taken away too soon
He too late

#Desiccation

Dark irony
Taste of blood
Flooded
Swallow hard
Allow
A taste
Wickedness
My clutch
Too much
Taken
Wasted
Not a drop
Hollow
I stop

@Alice

Red queen of madness
Hearts like playing cards
Swirling storm scattered
The Hatter lost his head
Blood waters white rose beds

#Astralabia

Souls reaching across the sky
A bridge of glass tween you and I
Walk with me under moonglow
In the dancing mists where dreamers go

#Decadence

Closer than skin
Draw you in
Enmeshed flesh
Dissolving into you
My eager hips
Melding lips
Slipping into one
Come
Closer still
Done

#BodySurfing

It happened all before we met
Upon the shores of sad regret
Where waves of shame wash over me
A forgotten she across the sea

#BruisedPlums

Blackviolets crushed
Beneath the snow
Secretshushed
None shall know
Violentblush
& crimsoncrows
Daydreamslush
Where shadows grow

#NeedCoffee

There's a hollow in my head
I've forgotten what you said
Hallowed in my heart
Fallow field of broken parts
Swallowed by the dead

#Fragility

A heart made of glass
Transparency forged in fire
Desire in a cup

@3a.m.

Deep resonance of his groan
A moan of first pleasure
Measuring my fit
Azure skies through slits
We fly through the crack of dawn

@TheRightSide

Exiled to my side of the bed
deafening voice in my head
our song playing on repeat
Further still I retreat
underneath lonely sheet

#Peaceful

Rocketship mind

Antigravity chair unwind

Cosmopolitan cosmonaut

Mapping the stars

Capturing them in jars

Like summer fireflies

Or UFO lights

A wish in the night

To float away

Into inner space

#StenchofFate

The scent of Fate whispering of late

A lingering favor harkening

For you to cash in

To win your freedom from yourself

Travel back to where you begin

Where you knew what you wanted

Exactly as you set forth on this trip

Giving voice to your choice

Nothing is free but everything

So long as you can let go

Your prayers are answered

Forgive me but you wove this future

I simply told you so

#TeamEdward

Vessels empty

She falls to the floor

Ghostly pallor

Breathing no more

Self-infliction

His lifeblood pours

Ruby lips

She screams for more

Changed forever

Hungrier than e'er before

Eternal life

A gift at death's door

True love's kiss

Morte de amour

#BeautifulBrooch

There is a girl of whom I wrote

She wore the softest velvet coat

One single rose on lapel was pinned

A poison thorn was hid within

Strong enough to steal their breath

Absorbing the smallest drop of death

And so many in this world depart

Being fool enough to touch her heart

#Late

Rocking me gently

Slow and deep

The subtle cadence

Hushed in deference to sleep

The comforting quietude

Like rhythmic sheep

#Feminism

From the ashes of our ancestors we rise

The womb of the Earth, the great divine

Birthing forth humanity in ecstatic cries

Asking for little but justice as our prize

#CastingtheBones

You can read his future in my scattered bones

My elusive heart now a shattered rune stone

Erratic memories of love now but a ghostly moan

Leaving him stumbling on his path back home

Tossed across the table by a wise old crone

#SpiritAnimal

Dream quest unrest

His demons made manifest

In bloody fields of poppy blooms

Woven skeins on shadow looms

Beneath indigo moon that drums

Shaman's whisper - cicadas hum

Dancing spirals as he comes

The beast of beauty and of rage

Token of his heritage

Silver sleek he lashes out

Fur on flesh with mighty shout

The beast now his counterpart

Living inside his warrior heart

#Germophobia

Sterile

Stark

Fluorescent bright

Linoleum white

Matching chair despair

Odor of death

Holding my breath

Warding

A cough beside me

Done for

#TwitterPoetsBeLike

Average cup of Joes

Mediocre prose

Decaffeinated

Morose

Seeking always seeking

Followers

Hollowers

Empty

River written

So few words

Absurd

#CreepersGonnaCreep

Stranger in an alley

Familiar facade

Of crumbling mortar

Worn brick walls

Want some candy dumpster dandy?

Chance encounter

With my shadow

#Caturday

Chicken soup comfortable

Rain pitter-pat

Daydream perfection

Just me and my cat

#ItCan'tRainAllTheTime

Dark gloomy day

Bedroomy day

I'll stay

Away from the streets

Between the sheets

Book in hand

Traveling a land

Sunny and distant

#MostImportantly

Breakfast in a diner

A metaphor for lifetimes

Over easy eggs

#Whiskey

Whiskey sober

Everything's still real

How to deal

What to feel

Teary eyed

Over-cried

Over tired

Wired

Trying to get through

To you

I'm through

#FairWarning

Visions Swelling

Whispers in the mists

Foretelling

Spelling out the gist

Crow's ominous flight

Dropped feather meaning

Ghosts in the night

Dreams feel real

She had fair warning

Unconsciously choosing

The rawer deal

Tarot card ignorant

Come the morning

Scent of destiny

Fate is sealed

With a kiss

And a goodbye forever

To the other road.

#RomanceIsDead

Speed past ignoring

The dead carcass of romance

Left on the roadside

#Holidays

She sat there crying

Cleaning up the mess they made

Thankful they had left

#McMonday

Hashbrown on the road

Someone's forgotten breakfast

Now a mcsmashbrown

#Flow

I'm tripping

Dripping tears

Running away from the years

Chasing fears

Catching up on old times

Old crimes

Slipping through cracks

You left behind

#LetItGo

Synchronizing

Watch as I fumble

Fingertips clumsy

Achy

Stiff-jointed

Nothing more

Complex

Pain full

That simple task

Of letting

Go

#WatchMe

The quiet

Clock-tick silence

Moment's peace

Disturbed

Recollecting

The intricate dance

Of gears

Choreographed

Beating

Death's tattoo

#Untitled

I retreat inside myself

But there I see

The entire world

Not just me

#OCaptain

The games can begin

Jump aboard my pirate ship

The captain is in

Stop looking @ Me

Resuscitation

Is an unnecessary

Aggravation

Restarting palpitations

Into

Conflagration

No salvation

Self-immolation

Obliteration

Fin

#Crow

Alight upon me with inky wing

Whisper dark omens in my ear

A storm is brewing in the heavens

A murderer is near

#Veiled

I embrace the chance

To dance

With the devil

I know

Once more in the glow

Of hellfire

Desire

I grin

Bearing

The weight of our sin

#Verse

I awaken with tears in my eyes

I can't remember the dream

But I can remember your lies

Why didn't you wake me

When you heard my cries

@Dinner

Memories like acid on my skin

Washing away the patina of years

Melting my resolve to stay distant

I dissolve in pain persistent

Reminiscent

#Untitled

Don't tell me I'm wrong

Let me foolishly love you

And fall in regret

#MicroWaves

Tear streaked windowpane

Slickened streets with no one there

Just the pounding of the rain

And the whisper of despair

#WinnerWinnerChickenDinner

Her life is dirty streets & filthy sheets

Grimy grasping fingers

And scars that stain her soul

For her there is no silver lining

#Muse-ic

The music reached in

And grabbed my still beating heart

And caressed my pain

#Wounded

We are all wounded

Animals on the food chain

Predatory in our love

#IceBurgLetUs

your promise

broke

my heart

the ice

between us

an ocean

apart

we drift

off to sleep

in dreams

we meet

our end

again

we brake

and break

away

#ShadesOfGreyGoose

I fall to my knees before you

A supplicant at your feet

Will you show me what mercy feels like

Or can your wrath be just as sweet

#SlapStickAround

Pearl white tooth cuts inner cheek

Sharp as the words in which he speaks

With a slap you taste your blood

With that hate he lost your love

@aVoidDance

She was pure nothingness

Perfect in her darkness

Tainted only

By the light he shone

#Kindling

From flicker to flame

Kindled bright

Ignited by kisses

Placed just right

How quickly it went

From nibble to bite

What will they say

If I stay here tonight

#Werewolves

Communion wafer moon's nefarious light

Mercurial promises of werewolf bite

Silver daggers with piercing blind sight

No rest for the wicked under spell of starlight

@theGardenGate

The flawless skin

Behind her knees

Elegant archways

Of ripened trees

Succulent fruit

On summer breeze

#DevilintheDetails

I am the serpent

She is my Eve

Fragile trust

Sweet deceit

A bite of moonlight

And poetry

@TheHospital

This old woman here

Scent of gin surrounding her

She waits for her name

Waving @ Children

A drifter came

Took their lives

A kitchen drawer

Rusty knives

First the husbands

Then the wives

Leaves the children

Away he drives

#BoatsAfloat

He never sees me

Miles apart

Adrift in a sea

Skimming the surface

Of my emotions

An uncharted heart

Doing my damndest

To rock your boat

The motion

An ocean between

Just trying to stay afloat

Rudderless

In my puddle of tears

Wind gone from my sails

Twenty years

Of bailing out a sinking ship

And failing to reach you

@13

Throwaway child

Defiled

Exiled

Tossed aside like a worn shoe

Ill fitting

Nonconforming

Mismatch sibling

Rivalry at its best

Failed another test

Counting black sheep

In sleep plagued by nightmares

No mommy right there

To wake you

Tell you you're dreaming

Dreams aren't allowed here

Wake up and smell the coffee

Love is a condition

For which you haven't been diagnosed

To them you're just a ghost

A haunted memory

Of a little girl

They used to care about

Vaguely familiar

#SummerBabies

The oak cracks its gnarled knuckled hand

Moaning as the frigid winds gust through

Snow-silence hushed over the rest of the land

As I curl up cozily in the bed I share with you.

For a moment I understand deep winter's plan

Everything outside has died, leaving nothing but us two

And as I am warmed beneath your hands

My heart chants out a mantra of "I do"

@ FrostFarm

We drove past Frost Farm yestereve

Gawping at the trailer park across the way

The neighboring house with sagging eaves

I wonder if that prose could be writ today

Would he choose to stop there on a snowy eve

As I had chosen to that day?

Or would he choose to take the roads that leads away?

#Accountable

Dear beloved of my heart

For many things I have much regret

I too easily forget my part

And leave you drowning in turmoil

That is mine alone

Like a spoiled child who runs from home

I know I fail to see the moon as I count the stars

Can't think of your smile from beneath my scars

I made my pain ours and hoard the light

Holding you hostage with every fight

You love me despite the pain I inflict

Now I stand in the eternal rain of conflict

Our differences fading like a worn memory

Lingering of the shadows of you and me

Just one kiss promises the hope for a new day

I promise to love you if you promise you'll stay

#thewalkingdead

Narco-leptic

Skeptic system

Nodding on the train

Fast track from pain

Light at the end

Tunnel vision friend

Riding the high

Grimly reaping lies

Cries heard on deaf ears

Tears at your grave

Gave your soul for a song

And the devil collected

#ValentinesDay

Corset tight laced

Hands well placed

A single rose caress

On gaping red lips

Hips undulating

Dilation of blindfolded eyes

Thigh high stalking

Stocking bound wrists

Tryst with a stranger

Dangerous valentine

Secretly admiring

Desiring to mesh

Flesh quivering

Cupid's arrow hits center

Entering her heart

@6:15 a.m.

Windup key turning

Thoughts are runny

Scrambled legs

Funny to see you here

My dear it's concerning

Alarm bell snooze

Dreams oozing out

To the left side of the bed

Filling your head

With my nonsense

#DarkHalf

She is my lemon twisted sister

Sweetly sick Queen of Tarts

Eater of hearts and pies

Queasy carousel of laughs and lies

Dark horse spinning fast in slow motion

Lost among distorted mirrors

No longer amused yet smiling

Carnivorous carnival of commotion

Beguiling purveyor of perversion

Diversions for the wicked wanderers

Wonders to behold. Be sold

Golden epaulets swaying to the band

Fringe benefits of being mad

Grandiose games where all is faire

Where sadness is a dancing bear

@theCemetary

I stand umbrella-less

In eternal rain

Today I move on

I lay to rest my pain

Letting my sorrow slide

Down to the mud at my feet

Sorrow's hold grows week

Like a prescription long expired

My outgrown shadow in the grave

#ShadowSinews

Her dreams were almost prophetic

The way she saw pain in coloured lucidity

A translucent thread that waxed poetic

Arranged in skeins of strange, macabre

And made her wonder if she could love her own creations

If that was what indeed they were;

Abominations conjured by her

To play out some inner wounding

A profundity both astounding and horrifying

Yet it gave her hope that she could change

@ A Barren Field of Fucks #IDGAF

In a secret forest

She grew her fucks

And saved one just for you

But you pressed

And pushed your luck

So she says fuck you

Now she cannot give a fuck

Even if she tried

You should have been more careful

Should've gave a fuck

Not lied

#ChippedPaint

A tire swing sways from the gnarled and rotted oak tree

The gray and faded house where home used to be

I stare at the dilapidation of the place where I was born

Garden in shambles, full of brambles, rusty thorns

Oh, how I thought I had broken away from my past

This has shown me how even memories don't last

I should've looked to them with more forgiving lies

Now the house has grown small and the ghosts have all died

#Once

Once upon a heart's delight was told a story of a night

 Whence something missing came to be found

Of a lady who loved hard then went to ground

#DeathandTaxes

Polar expression

Telegraph my pain

Rebelling against me

Taxing deductions

Internal residue of disdain

Secret disservice

What I need is irrelevant

Independent claim

Nothing is free

Return to the same

Cold calculation

The depth of a grave

Is measured in want

#Creases

Both balm and bane

Pleasure and pain

Sweet surcease

Of death's release

Like a silken duvet

Clenched betwixt fingers

A wrinkle

Of lingering ghosts

#Dishonored

Bottle fed blasphemy

Bred deep in the bones

Forlorn howl in the night

Dishonored, alone

#Playing

Lips of madness

Eyes of sadness

Taking him back in

The sin of forgetting

Letting him close

Desiring his touch

Even as you recoil

Pain too much

Loneliness more so

Can't let him go

Poker faced player

Royally fucking up

Flushing away today

For the promise

Tomorrow and always

Play your cards right

End a fight with a kiss

Regretting your weakness

Come daylight

#Imbalanced

Yin and Yang

Now a swirling grey eye

A storm on a cloudless day

#ClutchingBlackRainbows

Wrenching chasms

Yawning abysmal

Dismal dismaying

Praying, pleading, clawing

Gnawing at the bit

Fit of pride

Prejudicial rejection

Affection infected

I just died as you go

Clutching black rainbows

Alone in the snow

Peace @ Midnight

Let them not sleep the sleep of their dear martyred
mothers;

Disturbeth by the woeful unending need of her others.

Nor should they take the rest as their wearisome

fathers;

With the weight of a family on poor broken shoulders.

Instead let them slumber as babes lost in Nod,

For it is there that they dream lullabies sung by God.

#AntiBullying

Cheerful sun painted skies

Punctuated by pancake smells

Tinkling laughter of children

Tainted by coming school bells

And fear of a bully

#Forgetful

Butterflies war in the pit of my gut

like the effects of tainted meat

The putrification of a love left

forgotten in the heat

Incomplete

#2TearsInAKFCBucket

Anguish pours fatly from blue sky rent

Mere drops in the puddle of tears I've spent

Drowning in you

#BeingMom

Bury me

Beneath piles of laundry

And drown me

In dish-dirty sinks

Cast me down so far

That I cannot dig myself out

Wallowing in the grime of others

A person no more

Domesticated animal

Caged for too long

Tasked with the keeping

Of the habits of others

I toil away endlessly

A labor of love

#Witchy

Join the circle

Sit a spell

Pull up a broom

We wish you well

Tea and magick

Under the moon

Followed by chocolate

When the work is done

#Breath

Whiskey whispered words

That wither

What once was my heart

#Tired

Gritty eye-blink

Unsleep mired

Melty half-thoughts

Zombie wired

Dreamdripped mumblish

God, I'm tired

#FantasyLover

Man of my screams

Atone at my temple

Get on your knees

Take me to the edge

Make me say please

Bask in the afterglow

Then magically leave

@Bae

I'll take you to the edge of eternity

Let me atone for that love bite

Lay your bones by the hearthstone baby

And you'll forget your hate tonight

I know you can't resist the fantasy

Of my conciliatory pouted lips

Delve into the magical heart of me

#Time

The gloves are coming off

This love has made me soft

Time to fight for my needs

#More

Critical mass rejection

Electing to remain lonely

Accepting only the bottom

Feeding my worst

Casing scenarios better

Towing the line

You drew in the sand

Yet I demand more

#LimberingUp

Spine breaks as I bend over backward

Crackling of joints stiff from disuse

Limbs akimbo as I dance this limbo

Escaping from beneath your thumb

#PridesAdornments

My beautiful scars

Coalescing to a spider web

Dressing me in moonlight

Silver threads of healing

Like a fine Brussels lace

Old fonts of past disgrace

Adornments now of pride

#SkippingRope

Tachycardia

Throbbing moment I see you

My heart skips a beat

#EnChant

Circle of drums

The earth hums

Voices raised

Chanting, calling

Crescendo of yearning

The throbbing moment

Enthralling the women

The channeled Mother

Blessing of power

Like burning flowers

Brief and potent

#Refrain

You leave me bereft

Gifting me with fault

Throbbing moment

Robbing me of breath

Transubstantiating me

Into a pillar of salt

You struck me

A chord

In the tune

Of melancholia

A sullen vibrato

Picking at my pain

On broken strings

Like tiny violins

Playing my song

{Refrain}

Tone of Gee

You were wrong

@1a.m.

Opening

Wide

Astride

Fullness

Inside

Glide

@ the Rat

It was all liberty spikes

Of many hues

Riding bikes with pegs

Wallets with chains

Houses of pain and blues

Laced up combat boots

Kicking it old school

Behind the dumpster

Flyers for bands

Five dollar shows

Two dollar beers

Holding sweaty hands

No fear

Pit punch drunks

Getting grounded

Sneaking out

Tagging the bridge

Days spent at the Rat

Nights walking the streets

Fifteen deep

Borrowing dollars

Immortality

#Go

Butter fly

From frying pan

Into the fire

Of desire unmet

Patience

Not yet

Forget what they said

All in your head

Kick the can

Do what you must

Trust the plan

From the cradle

To the gravy train

Remain true

Do what you need to

For you

Fuck the rest

Mamma don't know best

But you do

Enough talk

Time to walk the walk

And make it so

Ready

123

Go

#This

This is the year

The year that I

STOP

Stopping myself from being

Being anything but

Me

@Midnight

Midnight strikes

And still I rewind

This cold device

Upon the screen

Your face serene

It reminds me

Of useless beauty

Like a white dress

Stained with time

And the bitter wine

I drink alone

Not believing

That you're gone

Advice Yelled @ an Old Friend

He only wants you when it's easy

Convenience store whore

Treated like a queen for the day

But who knows what tomorrow holds

Probably will unfold the usual way

Can't stay interested or true

Not when there are games to play

Narcissus in the garden

So focused on his own reflection

No recollection that this was his choice

To bail and blame the failure on you

Victim of circumstance. Never the perpetrator

Give him another chance

You'll be back here later

Doesn't matter if you're the mother of his child

Wild hearts can't be tamed or told how to behave

Slave to his impulses and drives

So he drives you away

In the end you're the one to blame

For taking in a stray

#Ode2Poe

I wait just outside

In sepulcherous gloom

With a bouquet of roses

To lay at her tomb

Hoping her dancing spirit

Will rise from earth's womb

And tell me she loves me

But I fear I am doomed

To wait forevermore

'Neath the pail moon

Here I stand nonetheless

As the wind whispers "soon"

#Melameaning

Two balloons

Floating to the ether

Pink melamine hearts

Filled with lighter air

Escaped from a child's grasp

Perhaps it has a symbology

Of which I'm not aware

#Faithless

He struck her

A jolt of lightening

Boom of thunder

Pain from above

Tearing her heart asunder

Her horizon fractured

Eroding her heart

With poisonous rain

Of his faithless love

#Svelte

He prefers his dice loaded

Not unlike himself

Top shelf gentleman everyday

Scotch and women his taste

A well-groomed poker face

Comped rooms all the way

They call him materialistic

The silk of his three piece agrees

Self-appointed king of all he sees

He'd rather put diamonds on their fingers

Than watch them glitter in their eyes

As he makes his farewells

With the prettiest of lies

Always the lone wolf

The cards the only pack in his life

Such is the lot he chose

When he took Lady Luck as his wife

#TheTimeTicks

Measured

In cups of coffee

And sleepless nights

Tossing and turning

Of the clock

I restlessly wait

For tomorrows

A staccato

#BannedShe

Enslaved by madness

In love with sadness

She draws you in

To consume you

Bite off your head

Take your for a ride

Get inside of her

She gets inside of you

Feral wild child

Dancer with demons

Stranger

Danger to herself

And others

Devouring mother

Necromancer of dead hearts

Obsession

She's a different breed

Endless need

Greed

Strip down to her soul

Dance around your pole

Ugly cry

Psychotic

Neurotic

Veneers are venerated

#DowntheRabbitHole

Descent into madness

Gladdened heart

Maniacal grin

Not coming out

The way I went in

As I lose my head

#breathless

On bated breath

I waited for you

To apologize

So I can forgive

Release you

From my heart

So I can heal

Exhale

But you fail

To see your part

I suffocate

On your silence

#NewYear2016

I resolve to be more resolved

In this year's revolution.

A resolution for lessening dilution.

Making this night an ablution.

An absolution

As I rid my mind of pollution.

A solution to problems

Devoid of the minutia,

And allowing evolution to take place

As I dissolve

Into my own year's revolution,

And solve the question

Of who I am

When I'm not trying to change.

@Stone

She could feel him hard pressed against her thigh.

Bullets and shrapnel whizzing by.

Scowl of focus marring his face.

Their lives couldn't end in this place.

Ammo was low, adrenaline high.

They were not yet defeated- refusing to die.

The slow cold fury of a shot rang out.

Dropping to the ground with a shout

Bound to Stone by handcuffed hands

Square on top of his chest she lands.

Seeing the hole gaping and bleeding

Tears in her eyes as she is pleading,

"Please don't die!" and "What will I do?"

Stone says, "I want you to know I love you."

"Tell me that later when we're safe from here,"

But stone was silent and didn't hear.

She knelt by his side and took up the gun,

Wasted the insurgents one by one.

She awaited the chopper with tears in her eyes.

You pick the end. Do you think Stone dies?

#LittleBlackDress

Little black dress

She always wears

To both funerals

And first dates

She expects nothing

But heartache

She hates

When they call her beautiful

Worn out spirits

In martini glasses

Empty

Dust coated bars

Sex in old cars

High heeled stumble

Fumbling

Into her flat

Echoes of home

Alone with her cat

Dress on the floor

A puddle

Of mascara tears

Vision of Light & Dark

Trouble brewing in her cauldron

An insignia upon a pauldron

Dragon descending on black smoke

The army of the Old One has awoke

A vision of warfare in the bubbles

Foretelling of the Time of Troubles

Defenses broken with a spell of sleep

All across the lands and castle keep

A single sorcerer would stand between

The coming hoard and the Faery Queen

She was the one to win the fight

Though she was only a girl and not a knight

Her voice ringing out on dale and on hill

Singing the song of peace and goodwill

#Wings

Descending darkness

Over body prone

Alone but together

Never touching

Shadows blending

Mingling

Skin tingling screams

Man of my dreams

Nightmare lover

Cover me

in

Miasma of need

On the wings of a tear

Make my heart bleed

#unbecoming

This writing thing was the first phase

On her journey of unbecoming

Like a butterfly tearing off its wings

And casting them into the fire

Desire to be more that what they allowed

A need to live out loud with her own words

Tired of being unheard

And unappreciated

Misunderstood and mistreated

Defeated by fear

Yearning to find a way to brazen through

Shedding lies she wore to become more true

Reverse pupation

A rediscovery of who

Unlearning the absurd hate she had for herself

Stripped bare of the should of others

Lovers, friends, family. Her mother

A realization of a she that is free

Revolutionary movement of being still

She can now just be.

@theWaxingMoon

Like the moon's first phase

A sliver of skin

Pale and ethereal

Her beauty

Teasing with promise

Of fullness to come

A silhouette in the dark

#Single

She was too good to be true

He knew from experience

Women always were

There was nothing he could do

It was only a matter of time

Before he'd notice the strings attached

He'd begin to detach from her

And her love would grow to hate

Blaming his failure to communicate

It was a vicious cycle he couldn't break.

#KnockKnock

Come!

Pound against my walls

Threaten to become my all

Promise to be my nothing

Lay siege to my senses

Break down my defenses

Invade my pleasure

Find the hidden treasure

Hidden in the depths

Of my darkness

Resistance seems futile

 But I cannot surrender

Your persistence so tender

Insistent and ruthless

The lines have been drawn

I can never submit

Death would hurt less

Than to become captivated

A prisoner of your love

Sentenced to die with the dawn

#OldOnes

The bloody and ravaged land healed

In a tree The Old One was once again sealed

Grain growing where the battle took place

Feeding the people with bountiful grace.

#Heedless

Tacit she turns

Lookaway lady

Refuting reality

Aversion to truth

Speaking no evil

The devil inside

Residing in silence

While the world burns

#StoryTime

I can't sleep again tonight

Please tell me a story

You know that one I like

The one with the mythical beings

With all their personal vices

That can't tell wrong from right.

Please tell me a story

Of how they fell madly in lust

But were betrayed by forces

Beyond their control of ken

But somehow managed to survive

And rebuild their shattered trust.

Please tell me a story

Of how they defied all the gods

Where was all powerful

And they found their happy end

Despite all the odds

Please tell me a story

That dispels all of my fears

Something to reassure me

That you'll be with me through the years

Tell me a story to dry my tears

#Loser

I fucked up yesterday

As only a loser like me can do

I broke your heart

And blamed it on you

I said you weren't needed

It just wasn't true

I've always been the one to blame

For painting your roses blue

I'm sorry

#CloseEncounter

He bore

The semblance

Of something familiar

Resemblance of a love

I once knew

The square of his jaw

Almond of his eye

Just slightly askew

But close enough

To do

@7eleven

Lottery Line

They clamber in

Line out to the snow

All for the same reasons

Myself among them

A clamor of wishes creating a din

Quantifying loved ones

In exchange for a win

Hoping Fate smiles kindly

The most joyous moments

Exchanged for cold hard cash

A change in their stars

A birthday or anniversary

The year of a first kiss or first car

Memories as numbers

The promise of a better life

Tonight we're all free of strife

Filling our lungs with excitement

Breathing the money in the air

The odds against all of us

But Lady Luck is among the crowd

We can feel her there

The equations will be right

There's magick afoot

And everyone wants to be struck

By a ball of power

#Unraveled

Go ahead

Pull the thread

Unraveling my heart

Naked truth

Traveling a labyrinth

Of my soul

My goal

The smile

Of my inner child

#Inked

Words we write

Righting the past

Mystic incantation

True iconoclast

Blurring lines

Inked everlast

Love is reborn

In moments passed

#Sidewalking

He's so slick

Like oily sidewalks

In a ramshackle town

A round for the house

Horror drowned

Rainbow puddle of poison

Staining the ground

#UnicornLivesMatter

I wrote me a book

An autobiography

Of a unicorn

#LikeLaundryOnTheLine

Light through the window

Beckons come play

A breeze carries along

Scent of a new day

My heart swells

With hope of Monday

And a fresh start

#Tang

Dark irony

Taste of blood

Flooded

Swallow hard

Allow a taste

Wickedness

My clutch

Too much

Taken

Wasted

Not a drop

Hollow

I stop

#Imogene

Beholden only to me

Emboldened and free

How real the taste of self

Sipping hate no longer

Poisoned looking glass

Washed in love

#DanceofUndoing

Beauty unraveled

An unrivaled whirlwind

Dance of her undoing

Spiraling drunk ballerina

Traveling widdershins

Pirouetting sins

@Isador

A note in a bottle

Washed ashore

"With love from home.

Te amo mi amor."

He knew that lipstick

Whom it was for

He whispered, "Isador"

#PhotoSynthesis

Turn away

The camera

Can only see

Just this side

Your good one

Unmarred

Unscarred

Beguiling

Half smiling

Play on light

And shadows

#RubyAmulet

The amulet of rubies

She wore

Faded to black

Cracked

Signaling the end

Her last breath

A sigh

As she fell out of love

With death

#DejavuBlue

Dejavu blue

The clock ticks

In silent room

The same gloom

Textures of last spring

In winter's belly

Disconcerting thought

#WrittenRiver

All the beauty she once beheld

Faded to gray and washed away

One drop of blood at a time it fell

Every year with him she stayed

#Beacon

She

The brightest

Shining scar

Morning star

A beacon

In black

Winter solstice sky

Twinkling light

She is the darkness

In my heart

#Crystaline

Frost giants waken

Yawning winter

Igniting cold flame

In my heart

Crystalizing our love

Freezing this moment

A revenant moon above

Bursting @the seams

Soldering

Smoldering

Held together

Welded seems

Steamy

Acetylene dreams

Riveted

Feel me

Coldsteel parts

Melted titanium heart

#sketchy

Graceful fingers moving

Over brow & cheek

Coal seducing paper

A caress from afar

Waking her

Capturing her smile

As she steps off the bus

@Dawn

Deep resonance of his groan

A moan of first pleasure

Measuring my fit

Azure skies through slits

We fly through the crack of dawn

@Moonrise

La triste lune

A wolf who lost his mate

Her countenance in the moon

Howling at the fates

She was taken away too soon

He too late

#Forgetful

There's a hollow in my head

I've forgotten what you said

Hallowed in my heart

Fallow field of broken parts

Swallowed by the dead

#ItPutstheLotionOnItself

Love rubbed raw

Chafed and sore

Still wanting more

Passion inflamed

Swollen lips claimed

Like a moth drawn

Carnal conflagration

#MisplacedKeys

Turned out in the bitter cold

Knuckles crack with each knock

The icy pain turns to numbness

As I wait for you to undo the lock

#Honesty

Inhibition tossed aside

Took the ride

Tried to warn you

You thought I lied

More's the pity

#Haikunamatata

Her blue morning eyes

Hinting at youth gone by

Apples withered dry

#LifeSaver

An old washed out pickle jar

Dirty change fills the hourglass

Marking down the days 'til he can go far

Paying his way with crumpled ones

@Solstice

Smell the crocus beneath the earth

Bunnies dance with joyous mirth

And robins sing for all they're worth

In celebration of the sun's rebirth

#StoryofMyLife

Nothing left for me

Except dregs at the bottom

Not even a sip

#DeathBreath

Never again

Will I be she

This woman

Each breath

A death

Of who I was

And birth of who I am

Who I'll be

#claustrophobia

I crouch hidden

In narrow darkness

Unbidden chatter of mice

My breath too loud in my ears

As I wait for the man

To abandon me

#FaceChangingTimes

The inter-netted web of lies

Where bookended faces have two sides

And birdies tweet but wolves reply

#Untitled

Divine providence

Promiscuous promises

Of proud destinies

#Rekindled

Believe

The impossible

Whispering wild

Dreamscapes of desire

The fire of purpose

Designed divinely

Eyes of a child

Reach blindly

?

Unintelligible fright

The living daylight has fled

Remaining only the dead

Afternoons of silence

All the walls papered red

#CarefulWhatYouWish4

She wanted her stars to change

For fate to be rearranged

Innocent wish turned strange

As it meant his goodbye

#Wounded1

Rose blooms from fresh cut

Blossoming on her shirtfront

Bouquet of heartache

#ThreadTheNeedle

When you fall apart

But allow just a brief cry

Stuff it all back inside

And hastily sew on a smile

And blink your eyes

Like a good dolly

#Please

If this darkness will but release me

I will go bleary eyed to the light

And stumble along the brighter paths

Than the craggier ones of night

#YourChoice

If I am your muse

Then you must always refuse

To see in daylight

#DisturbingDream

Last night I dreamt I was at your wake

I made a speech of all you meant

Alas my voice did not carry very far

So I was alone in my deep lament

#Close

Bringing you to mind

I feel a sting in my eyes

No longer a tear

#ImSoFancy

One of my best memories

Never actually took place

Twas just a young girl's fancy

That gave my heart your face

We'd never actually been acquainted

#LuckEU

I could've been anything

But I chose to be yours

Don't underestimate

My closing those doors

#WinterFrameofMind

The snow outside my window's frame

Tainted by shades of nostalgia

A blurred Polaroid of years bygone

Flashes of myself walk across the pane

#InstaMammogram

I thought I was dying once

Only for a day as I waited for the call

The doctor on the other end

Telling me it wasn't cancer at all

#EyeSoar

Your lashes

A gentle sigh

Of your eye

Against cheek

Seeking to speak

To the lethality

Of love

A pupil

Who learns to cry

At goodbye

#amreading

My misery-

Needs no company

Just solitary confinement,

And a good cup of tea.

Just hand me a book,

Then please leave me be.

#ASAP

Soon

I'll know

Who I am

When I'm not

What

You think

Soon

I'll be

More

Present

In my being

Less

Seeing

Past faults

Soon

I will

Become

Me

Soon

#Books

I want to read a book

Sharp and compelling

Cut me to the quick

Storyline swelling

Brand me with words

With a tale that needs telling

#SquirrelAppreciationDay

Squirreling away

My words for another day

To write bushy tales

#ItTakes2

Pull me to your madness

Cavorting contortion

A tangled tango

Dancefloor of disparity

Sadness & ecstasy

Comingling singularity

#BeltedOut

Strapping lad

Welts in shades of dark

Crimson & indigo

Starscapes on alabaster

Neath winter blue eyes

Glorious sparks

Igniting snow

#IGoogledCharcuterieToday

Rip out my cold heart

Delicious charcuterie

Of once passioned dreams

@Me

I'm too sensitive

Even with your careful words

I begin to bleed

#DissLexic

Dyslexicon

No pro

No smithy of words

Painter of the absurd

Jumbled head

Pull the thread

Poetry unravels

Sounds like a song

Spelling's wrong

Come @ Me Bro

I shall wait

For my nails to dry

Before I scratch

Your wandering eye

#CareBareStare

Taxidermy Squirmy

Stuffed with fluff

Care Bear stare

Call my bluff

I dare you

To push my buttons

And watch me unravel

@ThePinkElephantInTheRoom

Your ambivalence

Quite irrelevant

As the pink elephant

You rode into the room

I'm too far away to care

Orbiting the moon

In a lead zeppelin

#6words

Summer skies

Awaken

In thine eyes

#Elusionist

Miss direction

Special affection

Beautiful assistance

Show goes on

Magical delusion

Slight hand

Flash confusion

I disappear

Gone

#LightBright

Incandescent bulb

A bright idea

Back of my mind

If I check your pocket

I know what I'd find

May dim your halo

If I open the blinds

#HTG

Knees bent

Suppleincantation

Preying

For desires

Virtuoso

Begging

Small mercy

Release

Face raised

Heaving

Spent

To be touched

By His hand

@ThePrecipice

Broken edges

Of his vision

A precipice

Of tears

The ledges

He stood on

Every day

For years

Trying to

Keep himself

From falling

Again

#selfish

Deep down

In my selfishness

Lies a little girl

Who knew not to ask

Not to risk

Disappointment

Deep down

That little girl

Starves

#Wednesday

These mercies

Small

A single bead

On a weary rosary

Liturgy of hopes

Dashed

But for one ember

The rest is ash

Crossing my mind

#Khmer

She dreamt

Of golden earrings

Being given by her love

A sure sign

That she will be with child

Before the month is done

#IWantCandy

Goosebumps raised on naked skin

Sprinkled sugar with each caress

If you want to you can have a taste

Of my candy-coated flesh

#WastingAwayAgainInMargaritaville

The salted rims

Of her eyes

Gritty

Like the sugared coat

Of his lies

Pity

The essence

Of them crystallized

Pretty

Shards of love

#HeartySoup

You sought me

In darkness

Your radiance

Crashing

Against nights wall

We become

Amethyst dust

Scattered like stars

Across the dawn

#SilenceIsGolden

Gold

Fingers on curved hip

Brush

Gold

Lips taste her

Rush

Gold

Statuette of a Goddess

Blush

Gold

Her silence as he walks away

Hush

#FreeDumb

Ignorance confounds

Drowning in a sea of inequity

Free from constraints of mind

I find complaints for lucidity

Stupidity is free of charge

@11:11

It's 11:11

Again I wish

As I craft my poetry

After kissing my babies

Off to dreamland I write myself

And spend my wish on sleeping angels

#SingAlong

You the instrument

Of my destruction

Plucking at heartstrings

Background song

I dance on edges

To the vibration

Finely tuned

And sing along

#Gardening

Weeding out the parts of me

That grow needy and tangled

Strangling out the sun

With their barbs of self-effacement

So tomorrow can blossom

#AceOfSwords

Ace of Swords

Slashing through

Clarity of words

Intentions

The truth

Cuts both ways

In both

Its ambiguity

And acuity

@TheEmptiness

She

An empty vase

On pedestal

Craving fulfillment

Flowery promises

He

Brought a rose

Long ago

It died

She waits opaquely

For more

#ColorMeHappy

Paint for me a new life

Vibrant tones of vermilion

And indigo

Wash away my gray

With verdant seas

Of azure

And strokes of serpentine

#HighRise

Ego trip to the city

Pity that the buildings stand so high

Overcasting your brilliance

Scraping the sky

You're too good

To walk in shadows

#Frozen

Suspended animation

Salvation for a woman made of ice

Time is standing still

Will you pull me close

And melt me into a second life

#Untitled

Sorrow is a glove

She wears well

Black velvet touch

Of her personal hell

@TheEndOfMyRope

Broken ending

Frayed naught

Noose pulled taut

End of her rope

Cheater caught

Happiness cut short

Forgetmeknot

Untied Distraught

#StormWithSkin

She was a sea tornado

A whirlwind in her heart

Nothing but storm with skin

Chaos was her art

#Okay

Oh. I'm sorry!

Am I talking you to sleep?

Is it so much of a trial

To nod and smile

As I delve into the deep?

#Thoughts

Incessant chattering

The clattering of junk

The gunk inside my brain

Making me crazy

Keeping me sane

My constant chaos

#Mythical

Kobold

Channeling flame

To flight

A changeling

Of the night

His game

Imitating

Stealing kisses

He'd be mine

If I knew his name

#Cray

Melt down

The candles held

Into crayons

Picture me

A rainbow

From a frown

Smile pinned

To your fridge

A little piece of art

Drawn in love

#Thirsty

Selfiestick thin

Hungry

Gluten-free glutton

For attention

Approval

Laser soul removal

Designer baggage

Botox beauty

Anti saggage

No filter

#Swag

Trappings

Credit card interests

Plasticine treasures

Pleasure is pain is beauty is love

Only if it fits in a size 2

#Sleepless

Sleep is for the weary eyed

Not the teary eyed

They will not find ease

Until the sadness leaves

And their hearts become dry

I <3 Poetry

I want to swim in a poem

Float on inky tears of surcease

A release from simple pain

Into a landscape of emotion

Buoyant on an ocean of words

#Untitled

He is

The unspoken sin

That lies within

Her secret heart

#SongShadow

He was

A note unsung

A hum

Felt in a harmony

But unheard

A mirage

Dangling

On the edge

Of my mind

Unseen

But for his shade

#Chummy

I break

Pieces of myself

Fed to the circling sharks

I give 'til I am no more

A doormat without a door

#Diet

I need to lose pounds

Shed the dead weight of last year

Fit into new self

#IsPlutoAPlanetAgain

A horror whose scope

Reaches the sky

Stars crossing out

Any hope to change

Rearrange the planets

Ascend in the right house

Doomed from get

@Marketbasket

Guy talking loud about sushi

And being douchey

Just look at his shoes

#HipsterHeart

Blue-suede soul

Stains very easy

Too old-fashioned

For the times we're in

@aFuneral

Hold dear the tears

For the departed

The ache deep inside

Drops of painful brine

Your body's way of making room

For within you they'll reside

#January

January fire

A pyre of old Christmas trees

Sacrifice to spring

#HickoryDickory

Everything broken

Turned to ash

Lashing out

Spinning clock

Maddening sounds

Tick& tock

Dream of morning

Distant haze

Night bleeds

Sunny daze

#StandupGuy

Stiletto click on marble tile

Annoyance sways her hips

Mars her red lipped smile

He'd better have a good excuse

And make her wait worthwhile

#Artistic

Fine Venetian plaster

Hands of a master

Painting a fresco on my heart

Emblazoning my walls in sweet relief

My pleasure is his art

#Hangover

The New Year rung

In her pounding head.

A sense of dread.

Holiday hangover.

Spent all her joy in December

And winter's not over.

Sober.

#Pain

An overdose of pain

Lachrymose

Hard to swallow

Shattered crystal tears

Blood in his throat

Tastes like copper

Pennies from heaven

@TheLivingRoom

Circadian clock

Tick tock

The sound of

Fate

Knocking on door

Wanting more

More time

Forcing dreams

Destroying them

The dial unwinds

Too late

#BirdsEyeView

Went up to the clouds

On a lark

In your big balloon

Borrowed

Not stolen

I just wanted

To see

The moon

From the view

Of a bird

#SeparationAnxiety

The cold

Gripping

My heart

In bony fist

The feeling

When apart

From my lover

Worry

Carried along

On the breeze

I freeze

Waiting

For summer

#**Footsteps**

She bowled her way through

Footsteps clumsy

Fear-drunk

Defiling the words

And desecrating the hallowed halls

With her coarse disregard

#**Tainted**

His lips held the taint

Of long ago kisses

Making the moment taste bitter

As it shriveled my love

#Decay

My brain has rotted

Like Eve's apple

Left half eaten

And forgotten

In the sun

As she fled the garden

In search

Of new wonders

#War

Tis a new kind of war you wage

Not with righteousness nor rage

But with kisses meant to subdue

And falsehoods told of love so true

@TheHeartOfSadness

Dollydresssadness

Clickblinkyeyes

Porcelainskincrackbreak

Paintyonsmile

Mutesilencedcries

Dustyshelfforgotten

Childhood dies

But not for her

#NoTitle

I hope it dawns on you

What you lost

When you lose

What it cost

To not choose

Me

When you picked

Another muse

#ProseBeforeBros

Refrain

From telling me the truth

Youth wasted

Prose before praise

In a haze of confusion

Delusions you painted

Artistic con

#Seriously

Spending all my time

Listening to poems you wrote

For other women

Glistening tears wiped away

With a few choice lines

#IfIHadaDollar

How sweet of you to bother

Getting all hot around the collar

If I had a dollar

For every promise you spoke

I'd go broke

#DiscretionIsKey

Is it wrong

To keep lovin you

When it feels so right

Out of sight out of mind

Discretionary tales

Told by a master

Of deceit

#KillingMeSoftly

It's absurd how little you think me

When I can't get you out

Of my bed

My head splitting

Like my legs

When you sing me that song

#Str8Trippin

Burned tongue tasteless

Tactless

You'll attract less flies

With your bullshit truth

Than with honeydew lies

I keep trippin

Over your words

My ego's in my toes

#ThemEyesTho

Disheveled hair

Scent of weed

Look of need

In blue eyes

Boyishness works like

A charm

No harm

In giving in

A kiss isn't a sin

Nor is it enough

#HesACard

Add another chip to that shoulder

More to lose when the cards are dealt

Always bet on the black sheep

Suicide kings gamble with their hearts

#Connection

The thread that ties us together

That magic tether that binds us

Silver cord connection

Reach across the world

Remind me how close you are

@UnderTheBed

I thought I knew terror

I know now my error

As I clean beneath the bed

Of a 16 year old girl

Who's into art and Dragons

I found another world

#WinterIsComing

Winter's heart

Lives not in

Coldest day

Nor darkest night

But here within

This tree

That carries within

Seeds of life

Sun's light

#SalvationInASonnet

I was saved

Pulled from the edge

By a paper angel

Singing words

Of mirrored sorrows

Better tomorrows

I will never forget

That poem

#CeramicHouses

Tis a quiet town

Under pine boughs

Atop snowy blankets

Its joy silent

Unchanged

Magic

Neath tinsel rain

#Nope

The wrong side of goodbye is hello

Before you're aware of how it'll go

Ignorant of heartbreak coming your way

No ...She won't stay

#Anxiety

Stuck

The wrong side of my skin

Trapped within

Clawing to escape

Crying out with inside voice

Whispered shout

I can't get out

Help

@TheParkAndRide

Condensation

On glass

Blocking out prying eyes

Condemnation

Sighs muffled against lips

Hips locked together

Driver's seat heat

R&B station

#GoodCatholicGirl

Finger in my face

Anointing with sacristy

Pointing out my flaws

#IfDrsSeuss&PhilHadAFightWithTheDalaiLama InsideMyHead

What if I'm not me

What if

I'm you

What if every truth is untrue

A lie to me is a lie to you

What would you do

If you were you

The world askew

#AtlasWasABaller

Who is he

As a man

If not a provider

Work whore

Offshore

No account Loser

Monkey-suit abuser

Dancing bare

The world on his back

Baller

#PsychicPillowFort

Third-eye rainbows

Webs weaved invisible loom

Glory and doom

Birth death love ecstasy

Life in full bloom

Empathic knowing

A curse and a boon

#MerryFuckingChristmas

I hate you

For

Not being strong

Being wrong

Addicted

Afflicted

Not getting out

Of your own head

Being dead

I love yous unsaid

Merry Christmas

#GooniesNeverSayDie

Born on the wrong side of the tracks

I lack the spit and shine

To dine with the stars beneath the moon

Always using the wrong spoon

#LastCallinCamelot

Heart betrayer

Obeyer

Of naive whims

Looking for him

In a liars faces

Ugly places

For a white knight

Mr. Right

Keep choosing wrong

#FailedEtsyProject

She has become less

As life has worn her down

Sands of time on diary pages

Rough

Smoothing her edges

An erosion of spirit

Cast in jaded relief

@TheWillows

Carousel of souls

Noble equestrian dreamers

Circling a painted sun

Funhouse mirror reflections

Perfection

Spun sugar clouds

Merry-we-go-round

@35

Only years banish fears

Years of barely living

Beyond the past

Until the years become scarce

Dear

And fears become friends

Freeing

#1WP

Despair

A pair of worn out shoes

Wet snow on the way to school

Life unfair, cruel

Toe-numb cold

Soles full of hope

An empty belly

Stay @Home

Get up

Rise

Force yourself

Out of bed

One foot in front of the other

Dejavu breakfast

Wind-up key life

Of the wife

The mother

#TheForceAwakens

The force

Of my will

A battle uphill

Outclassed

Outflanked

Outranked

Desirous outcomes

Never come

From laurel leaves

Or armor

#Whatevs

Crystalline delusions

No intrusions

Reality bytes

A kiss on the throat

By a shadow

Hold the hand

Of a corpse

A man gone

To foreign lands

#MonroeYourBoat

A diamond

Girl's best friend

Alone with a cold stone

She spends her days

By the window waiting

Watching sungleams

Daydreams

While he's away

#BrewMaster

Hasten here lover

Pull me from bed

Sultry siren's call

Your scent in my head

I am your thrall

Allow me to drink

And fall decadently

#CoveredTracks

Fresh footprints in the snow

The illusion of a new path

Covering up my wrong turns

Lessons learned that were unnecessary

I want to forget where I am and how I got here

I want more. To be different than before

I don't want to live in regret

I want to take back those missed steps

Opportunities passed. Given away.

Thinking you'd stay and give me what I asked

But you weren't up to that task

It wasn't yours from the start anyway

We fail together because I didn't do my part

Now I hope for a change of whether

I want to get lost in a way that

My careful nature will not allow

I want to drift wherever the storm takes me

Bow only to the wind

Make a change in direction

But I don't know how and it's too late anyway

The road is revealed by a passing plow

And I return to my empty home

Walking back the way I'd come.

Oh well. Maybe tomorrow.

@The Library

Eenie-meenie-minie-moe

Robert Frost or E. A. Poe

Sylvia Plath or Hemingway

Stevenson, Carroll or Bronte

Wild, Kipling, Angelou

Longfellow or Langston Hughes

Oh, which one will I choose?
I don't know. I'll ask my muse.

#CurvitureOfVenus

Demilune

Curved breast

Gentle swell

Womb

Neath skin

Fire within

Finger-touch

Too much

Moist digits on silk

Innerthigh sighs

Land of honey &milk

@Aunt Flo

Story told in the blood

Ancestor dreams

Childbirth screams

Trading tree climb

For womanhood

A flood of emotion

At the gates of her pleasure

@ High Tide

An ebb and flow

Of sides

Tides of change

Estranged and distant

Persistent

Push and pull

O the pull

To crash through your walls

And flood you

#Nostalgia

Old paper cuts bleeding

Rereading

Poems

Of young hearted fools

Egos bruised and overripe

Our last moments

A faded photo in my mind

Panic @ 1:37 a.m.

I worry

About the stars in the sky

If I'll cry

When I'll die

If I said the wrong words

Looked foolish

Mean

If my shirt is clean

Everything

#Rocky5000

She loves hard

Rocky

She's had to fight

From the womb

To live

To forgive

To forget

Struggling

Toward the light

For the right

To be

@RevereBeach

I built a sandcastle

On the shores

Of my childhood

Let the waves

Fill the moat with foam

Waterweed pennants

Floating in midair

Declared me queen

Until gloam

#LycraBoss

Sketchy at best

Dressed in her worst

Stretchy breast-cling fabric

Coming apart

Seems fitting

Ill

ailing body

for saling

a modest income

#ProfilePickedApart

A silhouette

Forget her name

No beauty without pain

Pretty face with no brain

Insubstantial

Seeming

Always seeming

Vane

Inane

Dreaming

Old age

#BetterLatteThanNever

BusySidewalkLife

HeelclickCoffeeOrder

RingtoneDrone

ScrapingSkies

CeilingBreakDealing

Sorry

MommyCan'tSlowDown

ToLoveYouToday

#Lucky

D'you believe

In chance

Care for a dance

With the devil

Roll the die

Make me cry

Make me feel

As you deal

Stacked deck

Winner loses

#IncidentalSuicide

I kill myself daily

With broken shards of mirrors

One cut at a time

A thousand

Bloody wounds

Words shatter

Destroying my reflection

#Bio

Charismatic

Prismatic

Light

Refraction

Chain reaction

Experimental love

Chemistryset regret

He begets

A monster

The mad scientist

Playing God

#Rune

His touch magick

A rune of fire on my skin

Branding me as his

Binding burning bodies

Until together

We turn to ashes

#RevitalizationOfACivilization

Graceful steel necks

Metal giraffes

Of the construction cranes

Destruction pains the city

Eager for new blood

History a plaque

Local economy

Nurses @TheAshtray

Medication he's been given

Isn't even treating him

It's not inflammation

He's getting false hope

#PeakABoo

Hide and seek

Cut through the darkness

That you bury yourself in

Hoping I'm nice enough

Not to peek

Speak of what I've seen

Pretend to be blind

I'm not that kind

I'll find your flaws

And bring them to light

To be seen

Raw. Unclean yet pure

Enduring beauty in ugliness

To be healed by loving eyes

It's okay to cry

@theExorcist

Fevered dreams

Red haze

Obscuring vision

Curing ailed heart

Malaise paled

Parted

Failed to endure

The first bout

Whispered shouts

Plague and possession

An obsession

Exorcising trust

Lust the deadly sin

Demon within

Beckoning 'come in'

Day of reckoning is nigh

I die

And become like you

Fangs thirsty

#Echo

The loss of him was hollow-

For he was never brave enough

To love al her parts,

Or to follow her

Into the echoing atrium

Of her lonesome heart.

#LifeisaCabaret

Her life is a sad cabaret

A play in which she takes center stage

Traumatized by rejection's rage

A costume of forced tears

A fearful dance with no music

@Beltane

Magick is gathering

Grab your broom

Chant the words

Sweep the room

Light the cauldron

Stir the brew

Underneath waxing moon

Grab your chalice

Wish for a boon

Pour a cup

Draw a rune

Drink it up

For highest good

Your intention set

Will attuned

Merry we meet

Merry we part

Merry met soon

Next moon dear heart

#WhisperingWaltz

Will o' the wisp

On foggy night

Alive with magick

Wraiths delight

Ghostly dancing

Along the mire

Waltzing gravely

Gas-lit fire

Absinthe gowns

Swaying smoke

Symphony of toads

Chorus croaks

Eerie green light

Whispering sighs

Of tragic delight

And misty lies

#LostFutures

I cry for lost futures

The torture of knowing

I never had the chance

To be whom I'm supposed to be

All my gifts are squandered

Left to wander the earth

Waiting for the Morai

To show me mercy

To weave for me another ship

That I will be allowed to sail on

Where others have passed me by

Drowning in destiny denied.

#HoldingTogether

I waited until the trek home to let the tears

Streak down my freezing face

As I walked in the footsteps

My laughing children had made in the snow

@TheBallroom

Pinafore perfection

Confection of tulle

A corseted hourglass

Counting down the breaths

Until I can return

To the sanctuary

Of my boudoir

Uncoil my coiffure

Kick up my heeltired feet

Removing this forced disguise

Of a society ball

Stick my nose in a book

And escape it all

#CuttingOff

I'm giving the gift of letting you go.

No more will I let you use me.

Abuse the word friend.

This has to end.

Pretending you care long enough to get what you want.

Haunting me with requests.

Favors on your behest.

Disturbing my peace with your unrest.

Putting forth minimum effort,

To reap maximum reward later on,

But there'll be no later on.

I'm gone.

I'm cutting you off like the cancer that you are.

No scar left because you were nothing,

But someone needy.

Greedy for what I could give you,

But now you have to get it own your own.

I've outgrown the need to please you.

I release you.

You've always taken me for granted.

Your view of friendship slanted.

A leach. A sponge.

I'm dropping you on your ass.

If you plunge into the abyss I won't pull you out.

I'm out.

Everything revolves around you.

We're through. I bid you adieu.

Namaste.

Now stay away for good.

You're toxic.

Demolition of the Green House @ My Street

On my street

There was a house

A sister to my own

They tore it down

For no reason

Other than that it was old

And not worth the effort

To repair

They filled the foundation

With debris

Just a scar in the grass

A voided space

A paper filed with the city

Likely put something new in its place

Replace it

With something pretty

Cheaply made

My mind can't reconcile

Believe it's gone

I think of my own sister

Her divorce

How it takes much less force

To destroy a home

Than it does a house

I ache for her

#Jewelry

Fashionable noose

Encrusted in diamonds

Black velvet box

Entrusted surprise

Present to the hangman

Twisted golden rope

Lace my throat

With your possession

Lariat my heart

With your finery

Show the world

How much you paid

To have me

#SundayBest

What we have here is a failure to communicate.

To enumerate anything but my flaws.

I pause to reflect on your lack of respect.

Esteem. Running out of steam.

The little engine that couldn't.

Wouldn't do what it was told.

Too bold to fit the mold of a society ill-suited.

A bad fit.

Distempered.

Glass ceiling shattered.

I'm flattered that you think so little of me.

I'll endeavor to meet your standards.

Wouldn't want to dispel your delusions.

Eluding the box you try to stuff me in.

Sly fox from the fable just another woman unstable.

Unable.

Precluding a future where I shine bright.

A star hidden behind a cloud.

Not loud enough to be seen nor heard.

Spine severed.

Chicken shit.

Head to the ground.

Yoked down by "You'll never!"

Rising up defiantly despite the fall.

Wiping off my Sunday dress.

Screaming out "Is that your best?"

Any day now. Any day.

I'll show them all.

#TheScentofDeath

Hand-painted venetian mask

Slender beak of golden crane

Crafted for ingenious task

Of warding off the plague

Hiding place for flowers and herbs

Was part of the design

Disguising one from the reaper's eyes

Whilst masking the scent of those who died.

#BruisedSkyGoodbye

The strong scent of coffee

Wafting up to her room

Lace curtains parted

Sky full of gloom

Mirrors bruised cheek

She promises herself

He'll be gone in a week

@7a.m.

Morning sunlight filters through

Glinting off shards of broken crockery

Scattered on the kitchen floor

A masterpiece leading to the door

Shattered dreams of blue willow tomorrows

The debris was worth the pleasing sound

The crashing of plates never used

Their silent fragility a mockery

Of smashed long ago 'I do's'

#Misspent

Bankrupted heart

Always going for broke

Misspending all my tears

On an ungrateful bloke

#Homage

Village to temple she carries the ashes

Of her fallen lover in a rosewood chest

Prostrate at the feet of the gods she lays

Begging to join him in his rest

#Heaven

Captured

Taken

To paradise

On gilded wing

Heated breath

Angel of death

Uttered sighs

Gladly I die

Raptured

#BowlofPain

I am the type to eat my sorrow

Stuff it all down in one great swallow

I fill the hole inside my soul

Put all my pain inside a bowl

Knock back a shot of salty brine

Pretending everything's just fine

Bitter pill and humble pie

Washed down with tears I refuse to cry

Should you wish to dine with me

It's Ladies Night, women eat for free

In Memorium of the Old Dogwood @ The Front Yard

I

Rock-a-bye you sang to me

Beneath the great old dogwood tree

So gently there you laid me down

Pink petal blanket on the ground

Twining fingers yours and mine

A feast upon the sky we dined

Spinning futures from the clouds

And hanging them amid the boughs.

II

Adult hand placed on roughened bark

Cheek pressed close to feel youth's spark

Secrets long forgotten told

Daydreams the smooth limbs did hold

Memories so painfully sweet

Rained like petals from the tree

The dogwood kept every thought I'd thunk

Holding my hopes inside its trunk.

@TheCrossroads

Somewhere back

I took a detour

Lost track

Trail of bloody footprints

Breadcrumbs made of glass

Scattered in my wake

I learn everything the hard way

The Bard's way

Making every mistake

Crossroad crucifixion

An affliction of the mind

Of my kind

Walking the path parallel to desire

Trudging through the mire

Poetry is rarely found on the high road

#BioMechanicalSoftWear

I drink my whisky from flat gorilla glass.

Screen saving me a seat at the space bar.

Designated drivers running out of ram.

Spam for dinner with a dose of virtual reality injected.

My best friend is a desk lamp.

Time stamped entries in my diary,

Open book let me grab my glasses.

Glare's too bright. Ambien nightlight.

FireFoxes in boxes;

Seussical suicide notes written with no paper,

No one cares. Strangers on the information superhighway.

Speeding past accidents and train wrecks

On our quest to go at faster higher speeds.

Fiber optical illusions of connections are

Happy birthday mom emoticon worthlessness.

Dirty laundry online in 140 characters or less.

ALY SEBASTIAN

United separately.

Web addressing the crisis in the middle east.

Feast your eyes on the pic of a plate at a restaurant you can't afford.

Plugged into the matrix.

Neo not see propaganda. Raging against the machines we bond with.

Siri added me on twitter. She's real. I don't care.

Like and share.

Baring my nakedness from the safety of my couch

With the lights tv xbox playsation phone on

Globally warming up to being slaves.

I need an outlet to plug my heart in

Saving my battery for cyber bullying others into joining my anti-bullying campaign.

A quiz I took told me I'm sane but,

Medicate me into numbness.

Dumb down my speech. Pain can be abbreviated.

Youtube terrorist videos with advertisements for

bacon.

Faking real life with gaunt pail children

Diabetic shocking photos if you just click here.

Outdoor settings on your camera

First let me take a selfie so we can go home.

Check in at the drive thru buying dinner in a bag

Reading comments hoping they like you

Just like you they're using apps to cover their faces.

Ban the bourka! We need to see with no filters

Despair over our list of friends from second grade.

My status says I've got it made and it went viral so it must be true.

Society's new glue sticking your face to the screen

So you can't see what's going on.

Fattening you up for the slaughter.

Books are dead! Newspapers unread.

Save a tree. Buy canned air instead!

#ComeTheMourning

I'll find my out

This pit of despair

Dug myself in deep this time

Fingernails black with soil

Leaves matted in my hair

Night is coming

I can't sleep

Fear of nightmares

And slithering shadows

Slimy with remembrance

Distantly

I can hear the wolves howl

Echoing my heart

Baying at the sky

Ready to tear me apart

With wild abandon

You left me

I'm not going to die

Not for your love

I must stay buried

Survive

Come the mourning

#Mad

My jacket is not on quite straight.

Please assist me. I can't be late!

I've a date with some dear old friends.

Down the rabbit hole I must descend.

To eat some mushrooms and have some tea,

And conversate with Tweedle Dee.

I must paint all the roses red

Or the Queen of Hearts will take my head.

The Hatter can take care of that

With a little help from the Cheshire Cat.

Please don't look at me like that my dear!

I'm a writer and we're all mad here!

Tweets from a Wounded Nightingale

Today I feel like a failure

The tears will probably pass

The fire in my solar plexus will reignite

But for now I am wallowing

Swallowing back tears

Maybe I've wasted too many years

A rusty knife in a drawer

Can't cut it

Overinflated hopes doomed to burst

Wouldn't be the first time

Such is my curse

Being a bird in a world full of lions

With broken wing and pitiful song

It always seems to come out wrong

Yet I keep trying to beat my wings

To roar

Or soar

Fly away

And avoid being eaten

Tomorrow is another day

I'll figure it out then.

ABOUT THE AUTHOR

Aly Sebastian is an artist and the author. Her three published works are Redemption, Clairvoyant, and Seasonally Defective: Poetry for Goddesses and Mortal Women. She lives in Massachusetts with her husband and children. Follow her on Twitter @intuitivealy

www.ingramcontent.com/pod-product-compliance
Lightning Source LLC
LaVergne TN
LVHW051231080426
835513LV00016B/1517